Drawing On

The Life Of Our Lord

following
a rough outline of
The Life Of Our Lord
written in the 1840s
by Charles Dickens
for his children

Stephen Joseph Wolf

IDJC press

Charles Dickens wrote *The Life of Our Lord* for his young children in the 1840's. His family published it in 1934.

It is one of several little books I like to read during long walks. Some years ago I made a rough outline of it for retreats and such until one Monk Monday was spent with that outline and a brush and some black ink. These ink brush drawings are from that day, with apologies to real artists everywhere.

Some of the drawings appeared in a meditation rendering called *A Jesus Breviary*, but I have often wanted to put them with the outline of Dickens' great little book for his children.

Crayons are allowed.

Rev. Steve Wolf
Christmas 2018

ISBN 978-1-937081-66-9

IDJC press
www.idjc.org

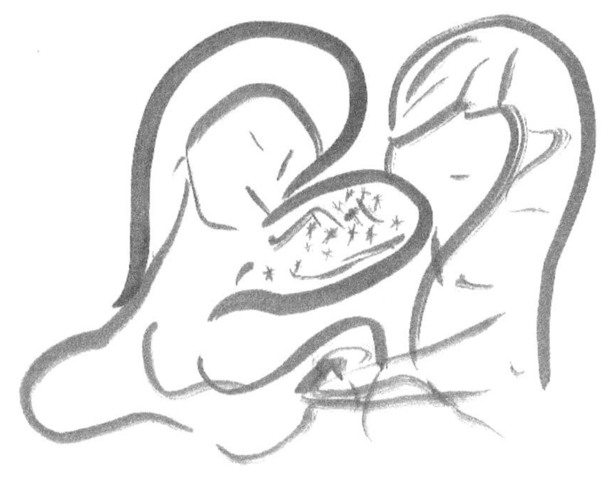

Birth of
Jesus Christ

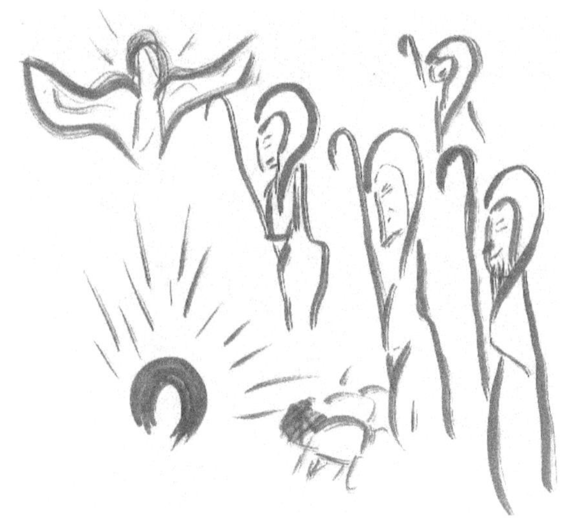

Shepherds
On Watch
in the Fields

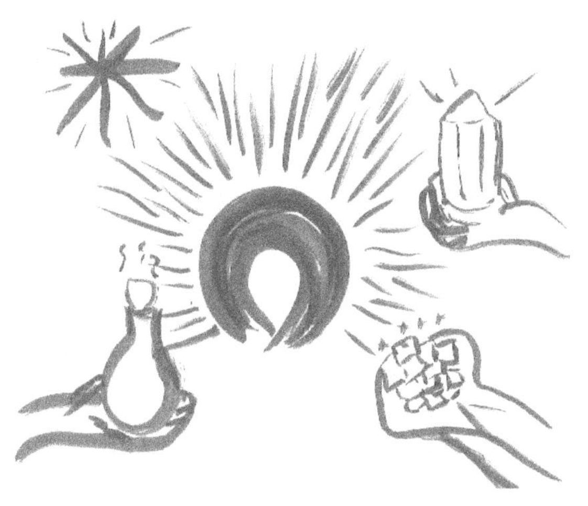

Wise Men from a Long Way Off in the East

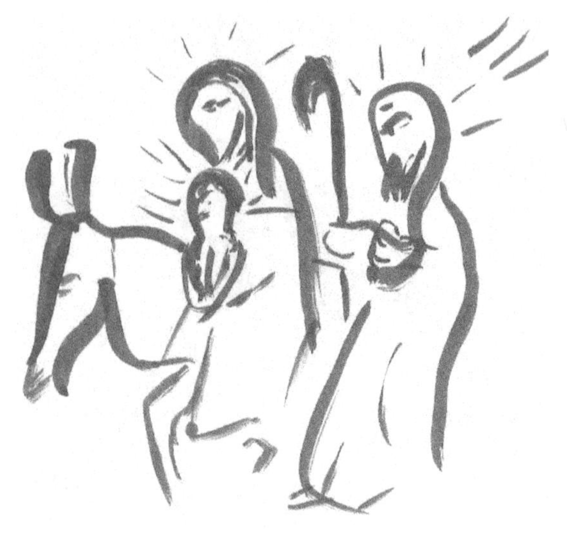

Escape to Egypt

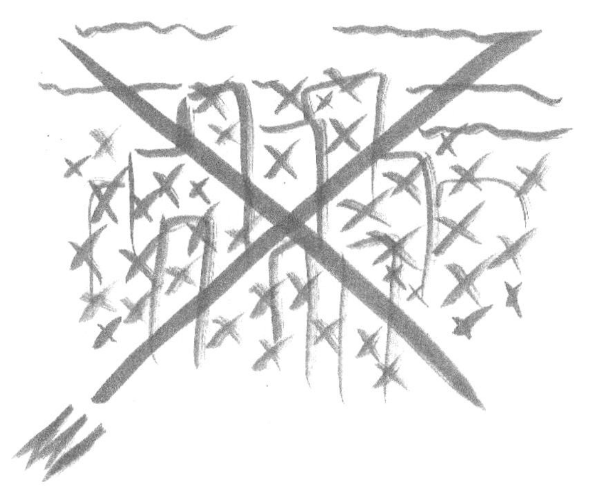

Murder
of the Innocents
by Cruel King Herod

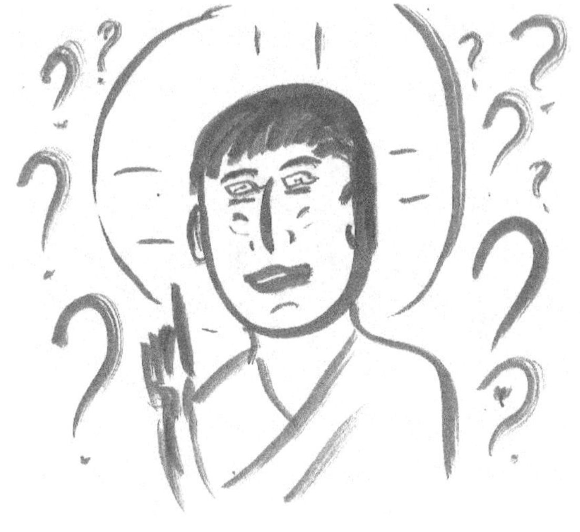

Twelve-Year-Old Jesus with the Doctors in the Temple

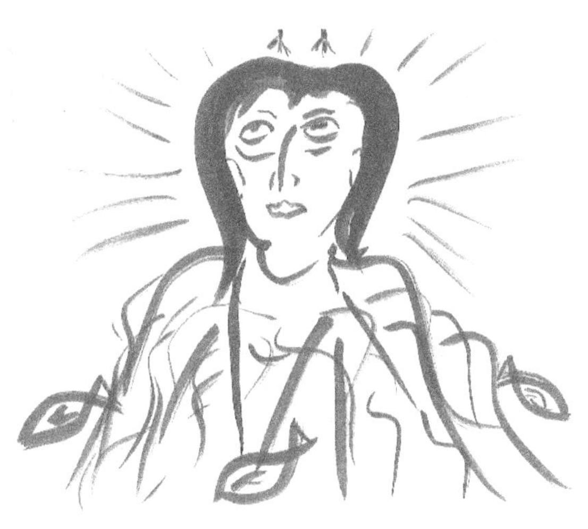

Jesus Christ
Baptized by John
in the River Jordan

Forty Days
and
Forty Nights
in the
Wilderness

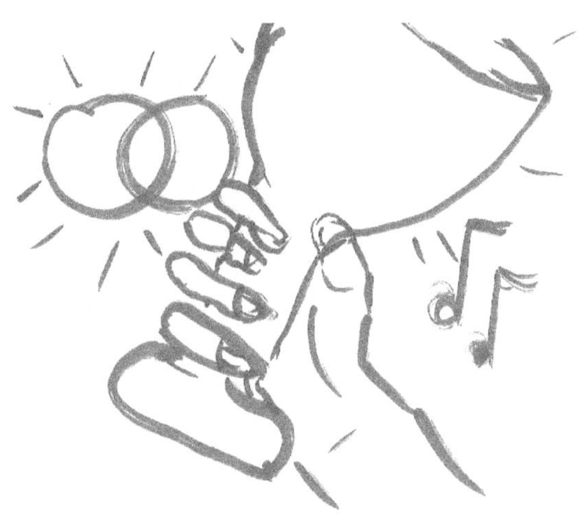

First Miracle at the
Marriage-Feast
in Cana

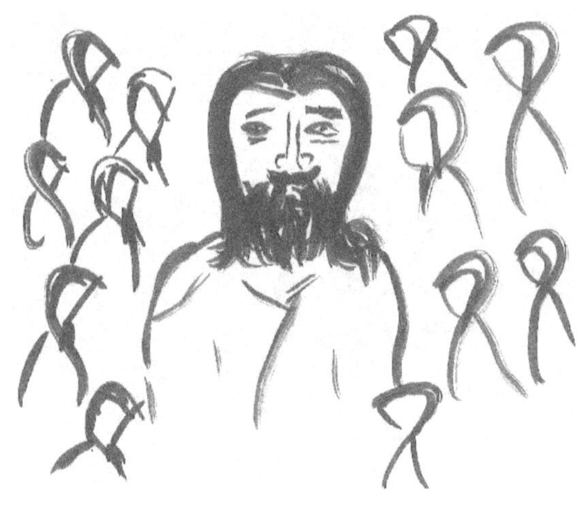

Choosing of Twelve Poor Men Called Apostles or Disciples

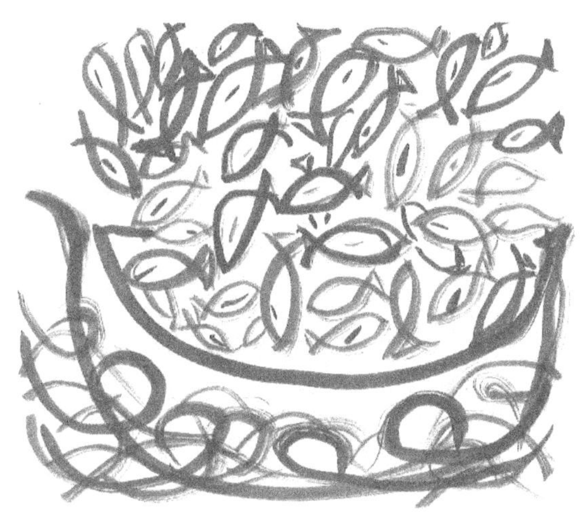

Net Full of Fish

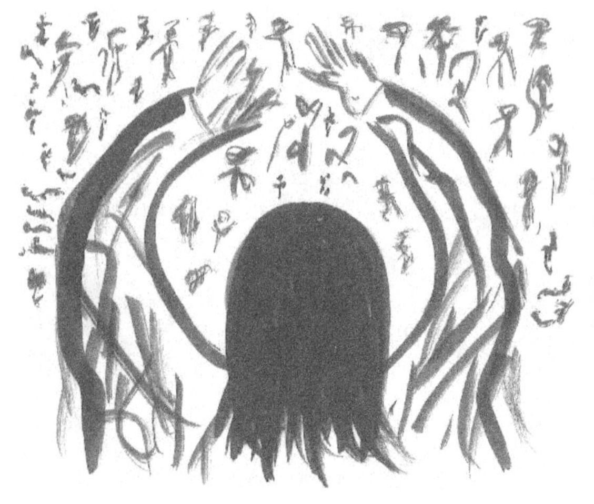

Teaching Preaching the Prayer that Begins *Our Father*

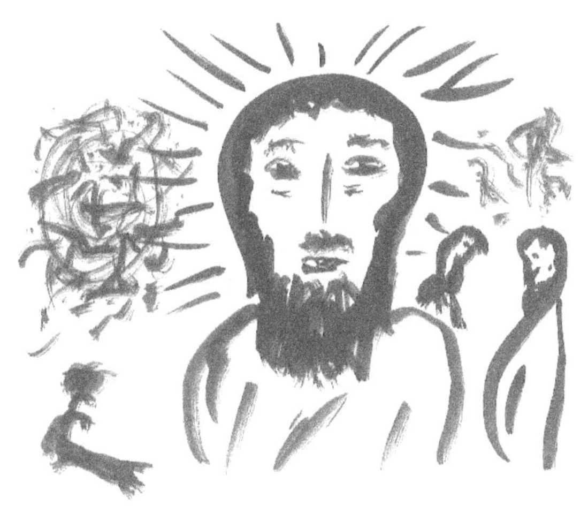

Healing of a Leper, a Man with Palsy, Centurion's Servant & Magistrate's Daughter

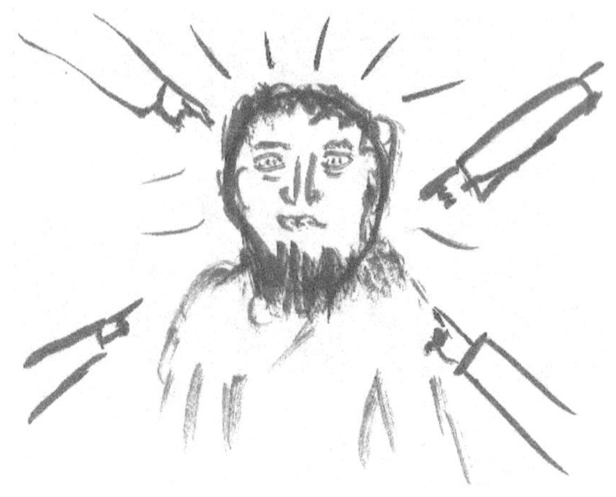

Challenges of
the Pharisees

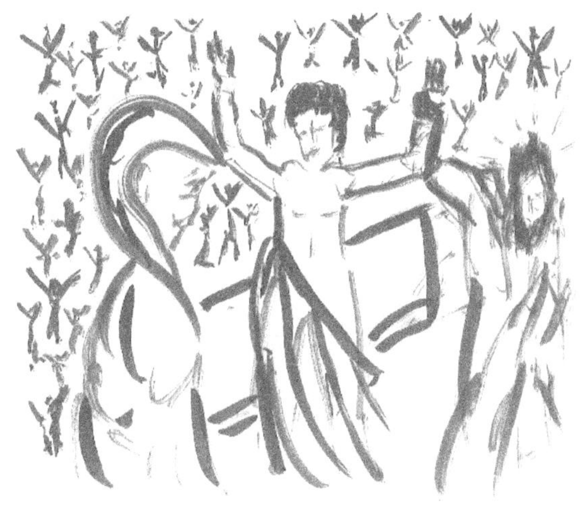

Raising
the Only Son of
the Widow of Nain

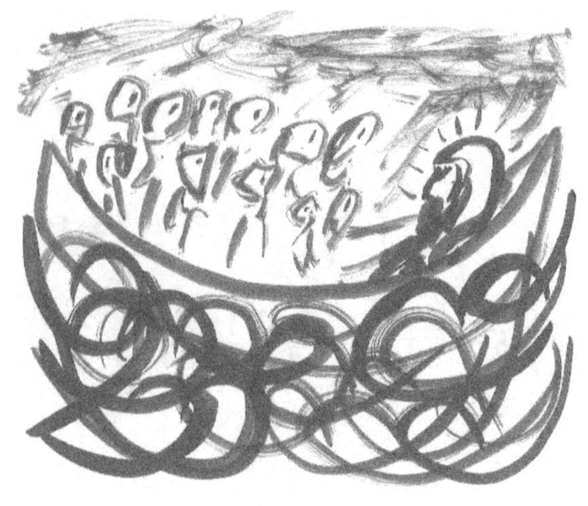

Jesus Asleep
in the Boat in
a Violent Storm

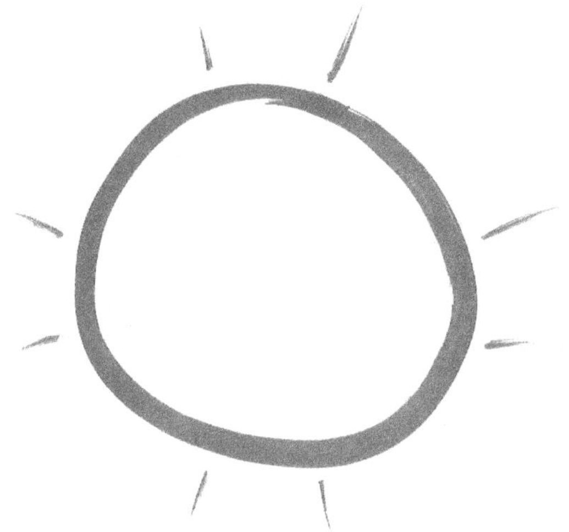

Jesus Is Awoken
and Calms the Storm

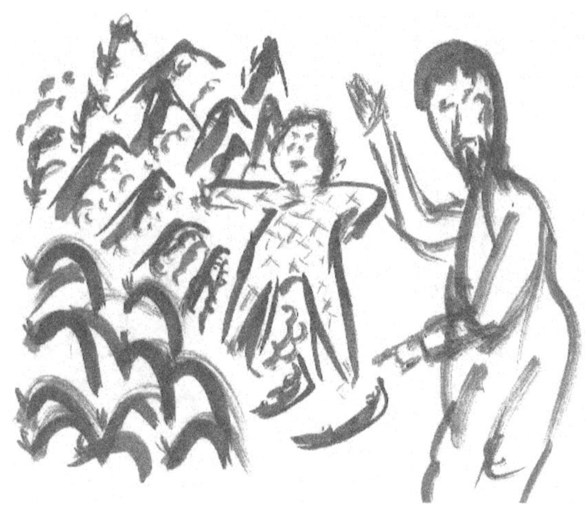

Casting Evil Spirits
into a Herd of Swine

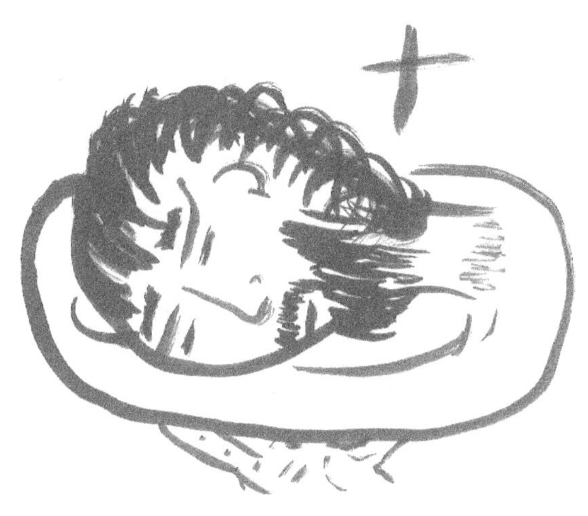

Imprisonment
and Beheading
of John the Baptist

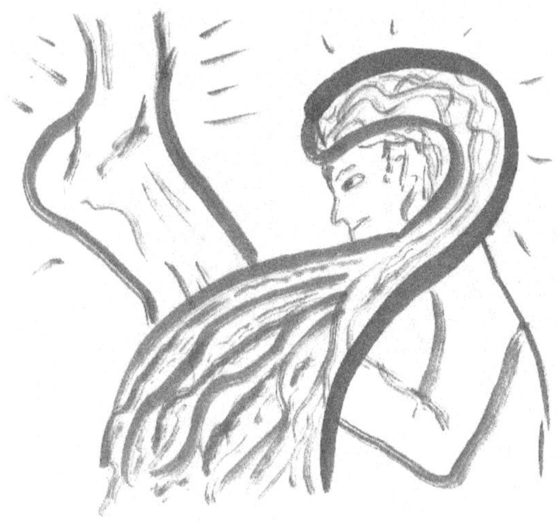

A Woman Washes Jesus' Feet with her Tears and Hair

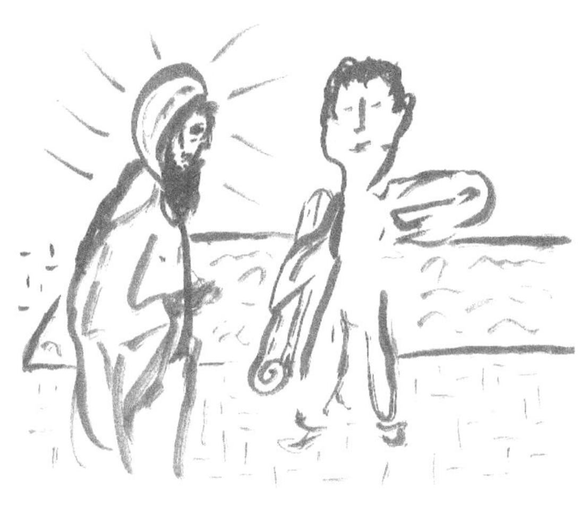

A Man Ill for 38 Years
is Healed at
the Pool of Bethesda

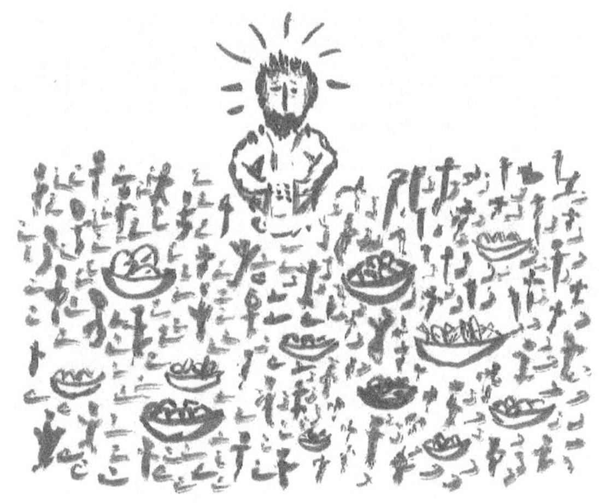

Feeding of 5,000+ from Five Loaves and Two Fish

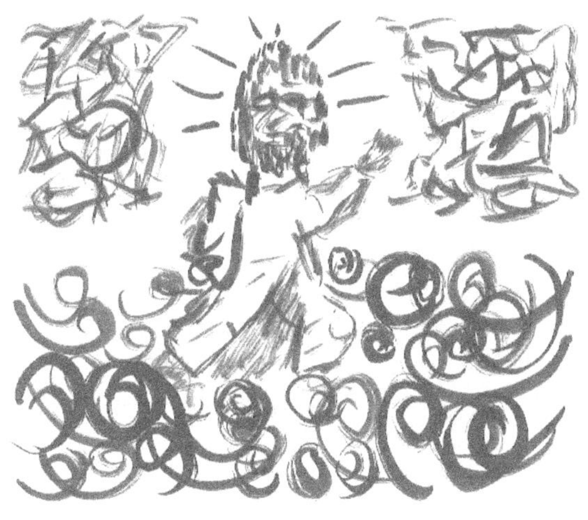

Walking on Water
as if on Dry Land

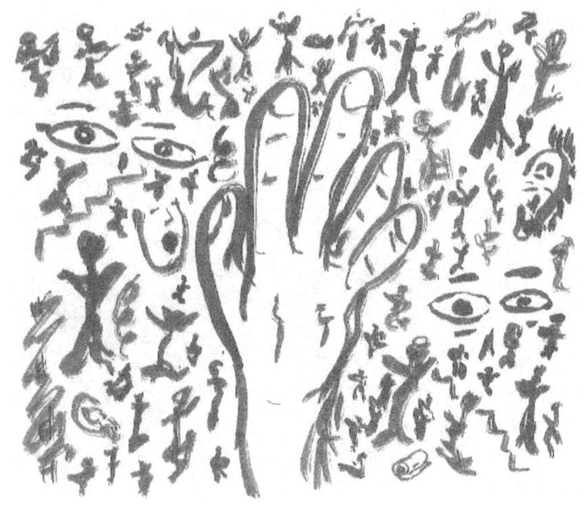

Many More
Healing Miracles

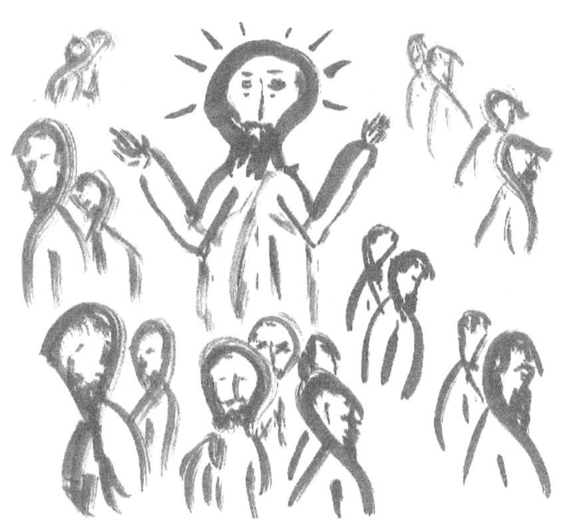

Sending of Disciples into Towns and Villages

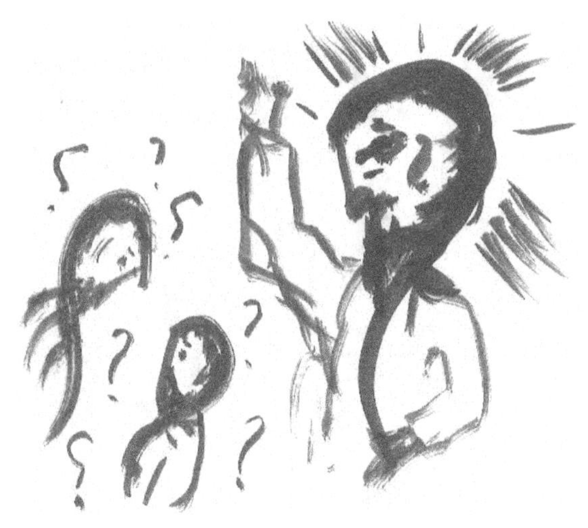

Jesus Predicts his Dying and Rising and Ascending

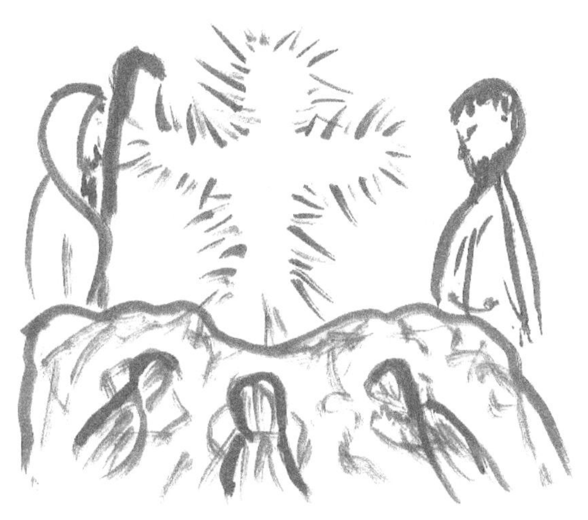

Transfiguration
on a
High Mountain

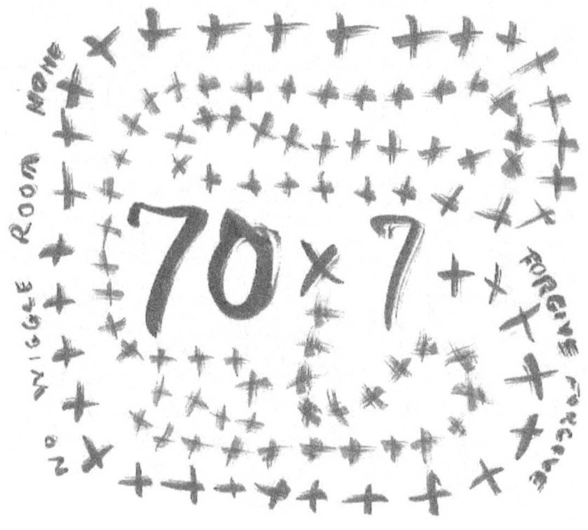

Teaching on Forgiving

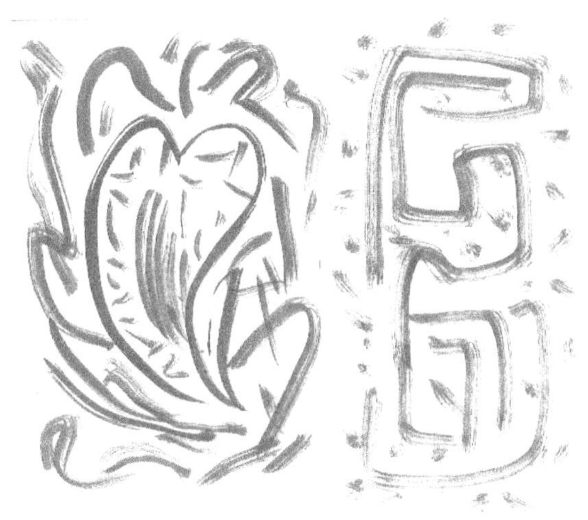

Stories of the Generous Master and Unforgiving Servant

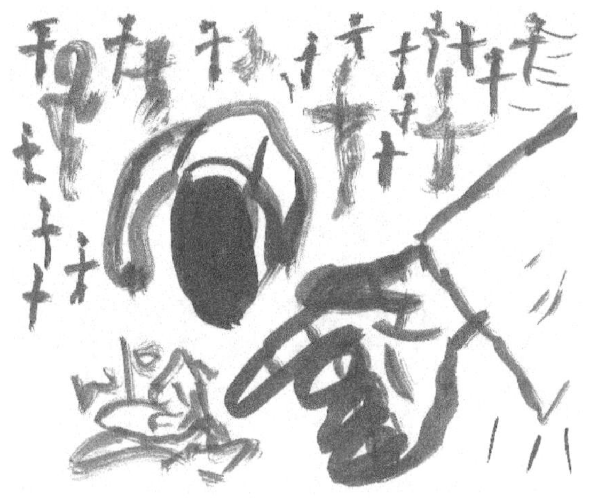

Jesus and
the Accusers
of a Woman

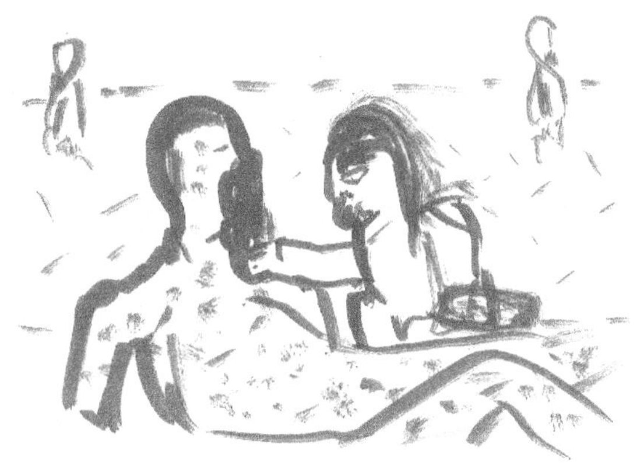

Story of a Samaritan Who Showed Compassion

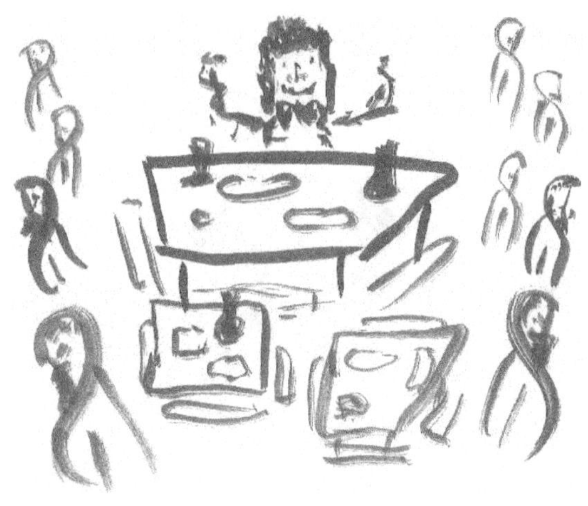

Story of the Excuses of Those Invited to a Great Supper

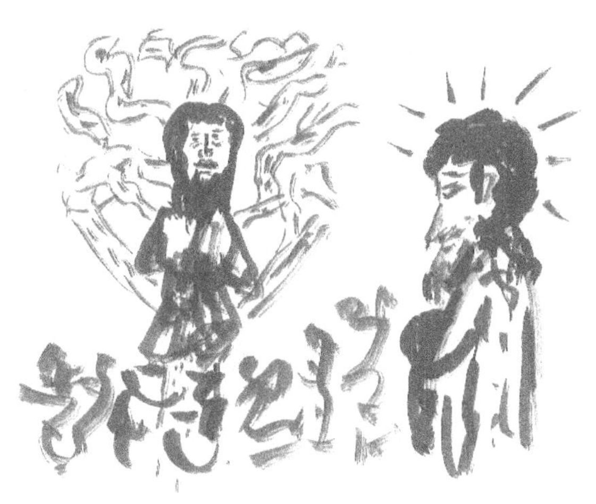

Jesus Calls Out
to Zacchaeus
in the Tree

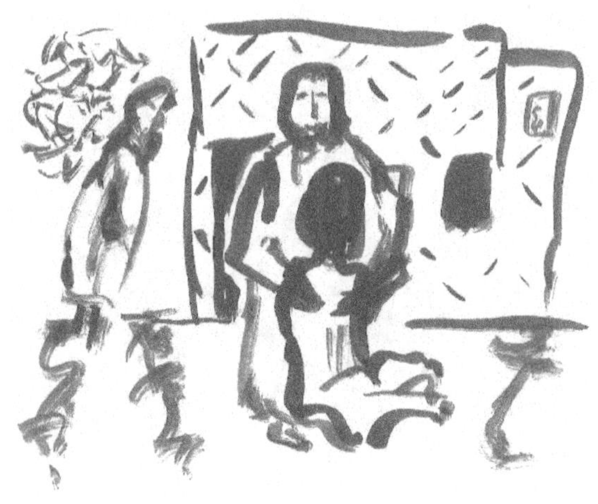

Story Usually Called
the Prodigal Son

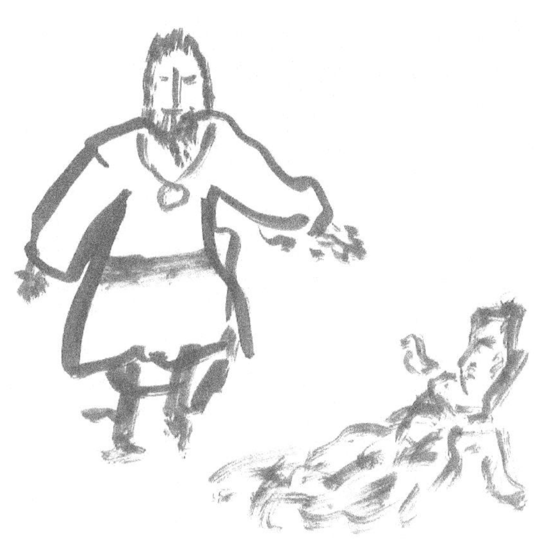

Story of the Rich Man and the Beggar Lazarus

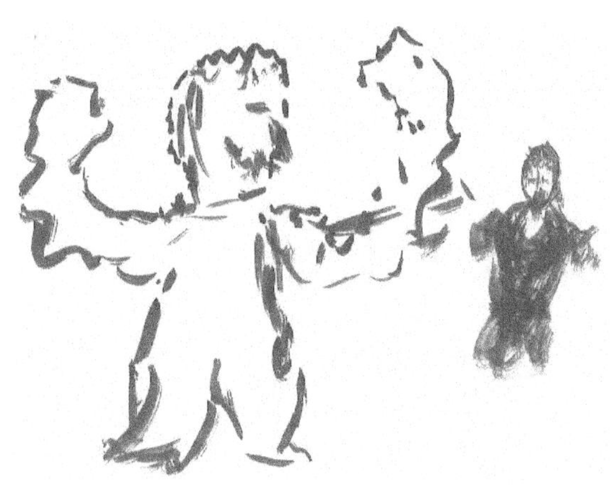

A Proud Man and
a Humble Man
in the Temple

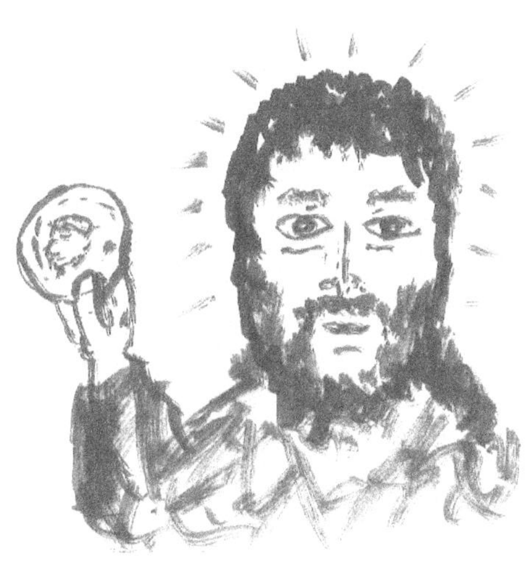

Jesus Questioned about Paying a Tribute to Caesar

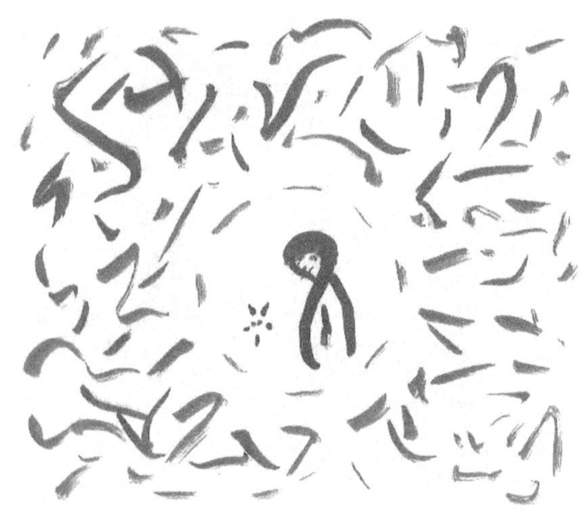

Example of
a Poor Widow and
her Gift of Two Mites

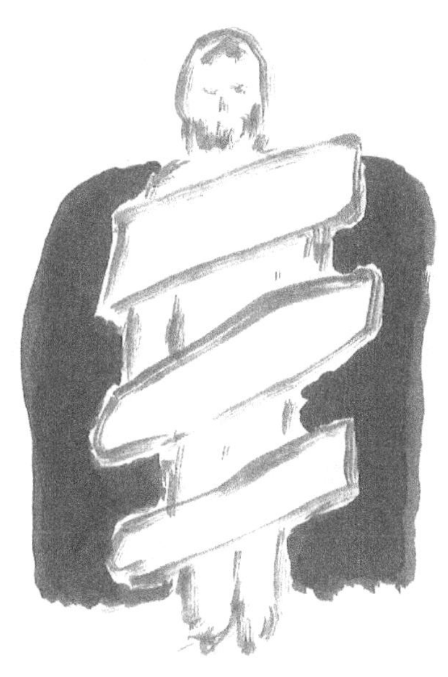

Lazarus of Bethany
Restored to Life

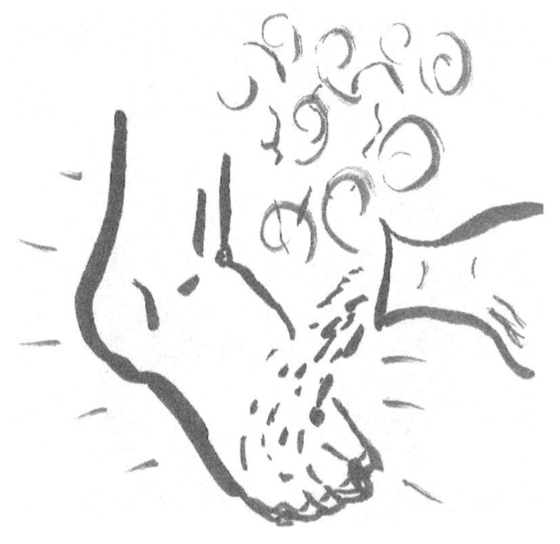

Mary of Bethany Anoints Jesus' Feet with Ointment

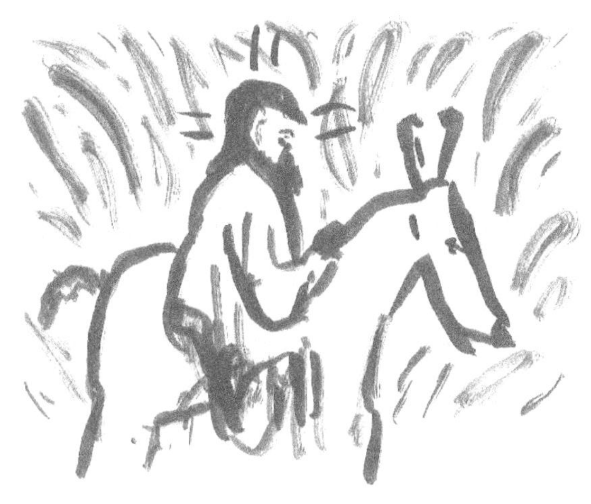

Jesus Enters Jerusalem Riding on an Ass; *Hosanna!*

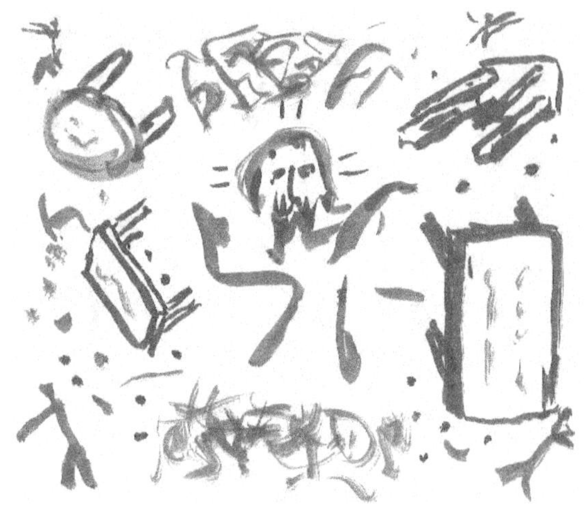

Jesus Casts Out the Tables of the Money Changers

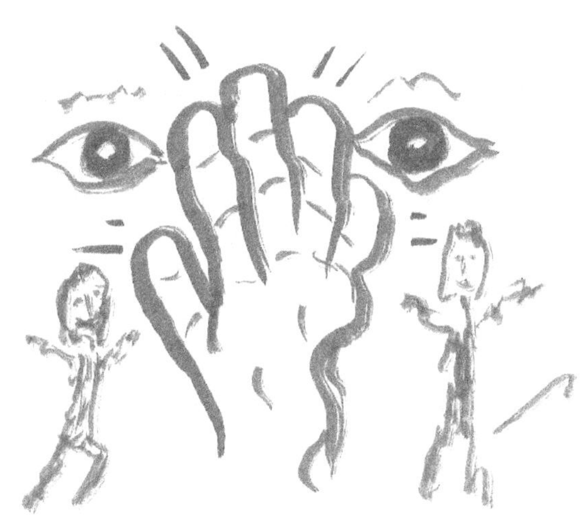

More of the
Blind and Lame
are Healed by Him

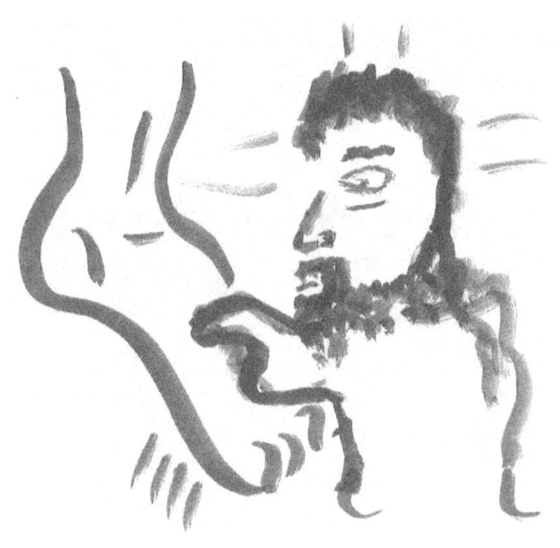

Jesus Washes the Feet of His Disciples

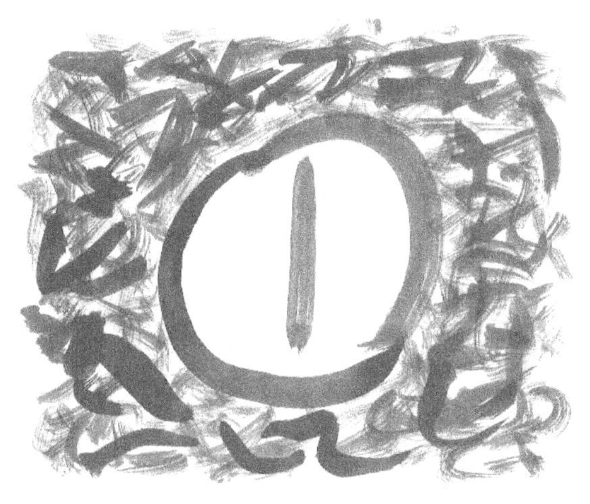

Jesus Says
There Is One
Who Will Betray Him

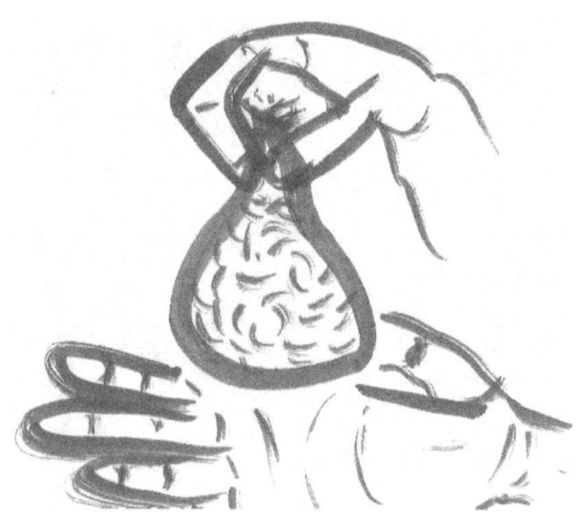

Judas Iscariot Accepts
Thirty Pieces of Silver

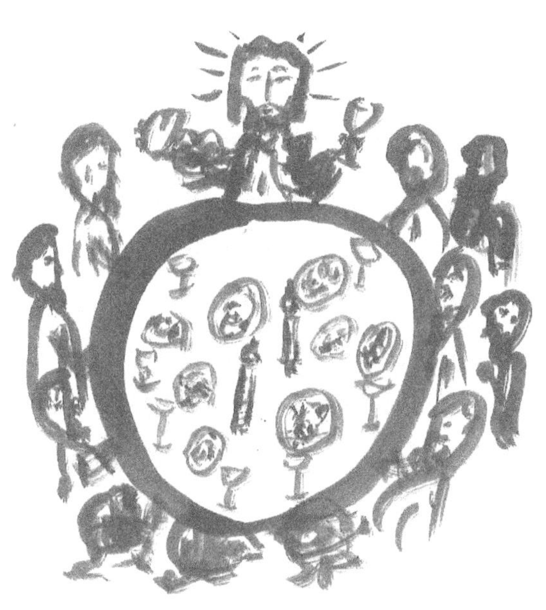

The Last Supper
of the Passover

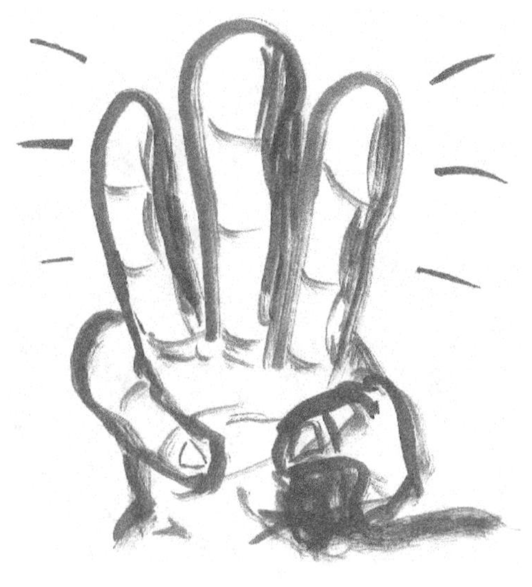

Jesus Tells Peter that He Will Deny Him Three Times

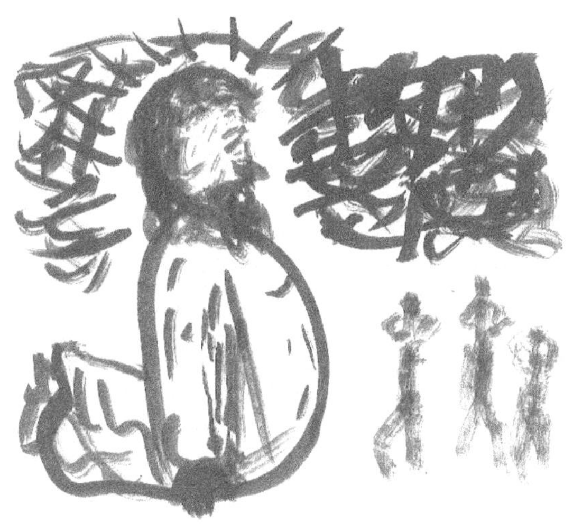

Jesus Prays and
the Disciples Sleep
in Gethsemane

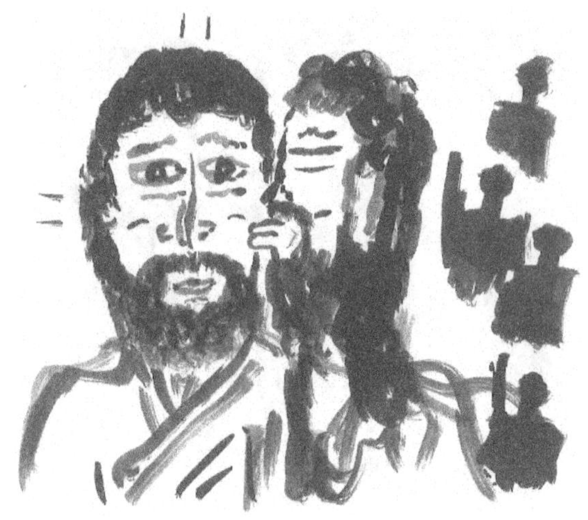

Judas Arrives
with a Strong Guard
and Kisses Jesus

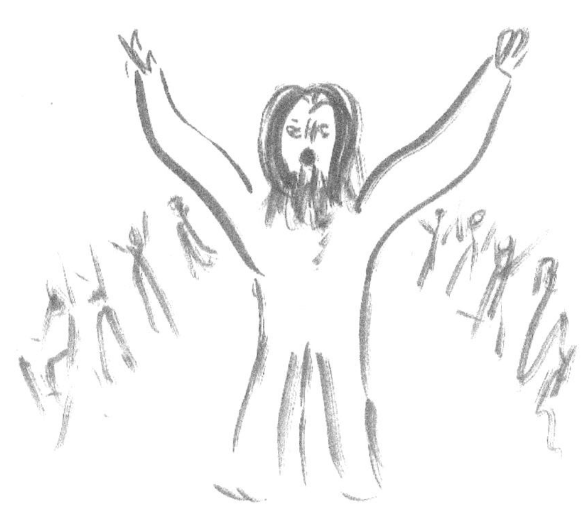

Peter Denies Jesus, the Cock Crows, and Peter Weeps

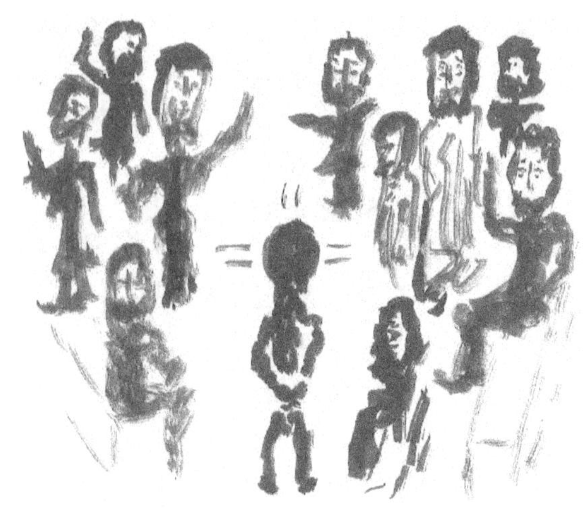

The Scribes
and Priests Agree
Jesus Is to be Killed

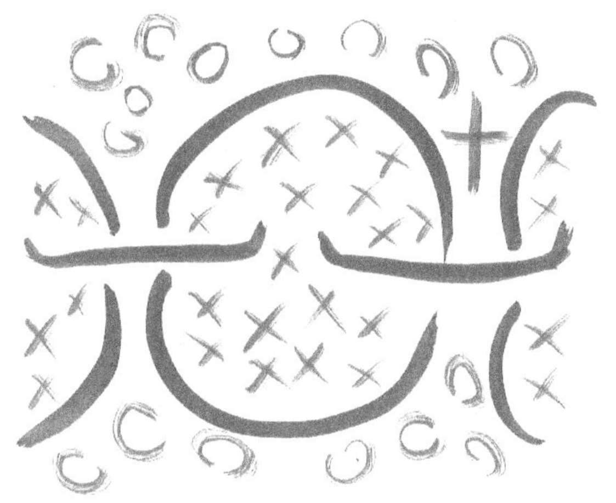

Judas Throws
the Silver Down
and Takes his Life

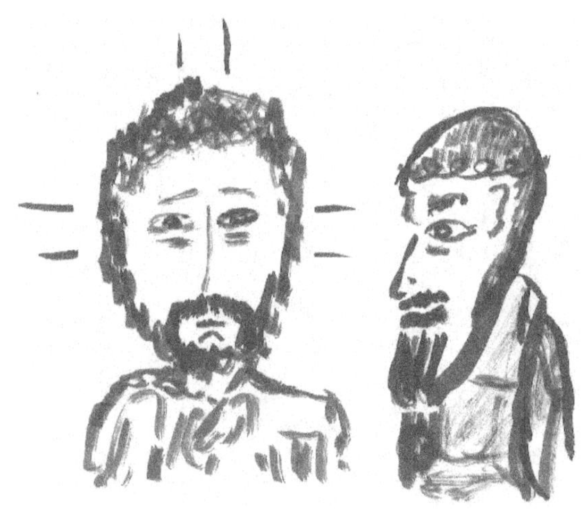

Jesus Questioned
by Pontius Pilate,
What Have You Done?

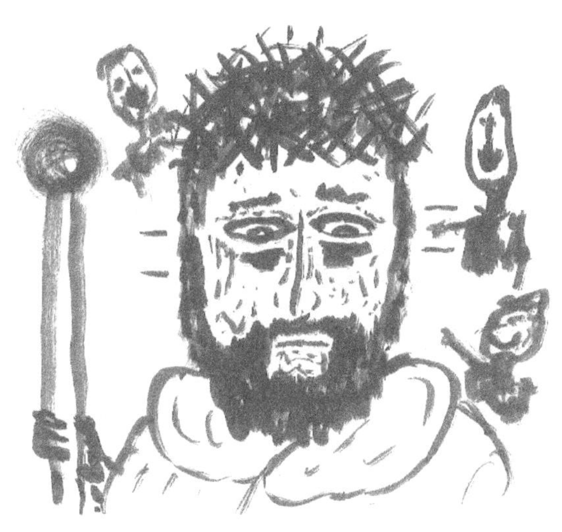

Pilate has Jesus Beaten, Mocked, and Crowned with Thorns

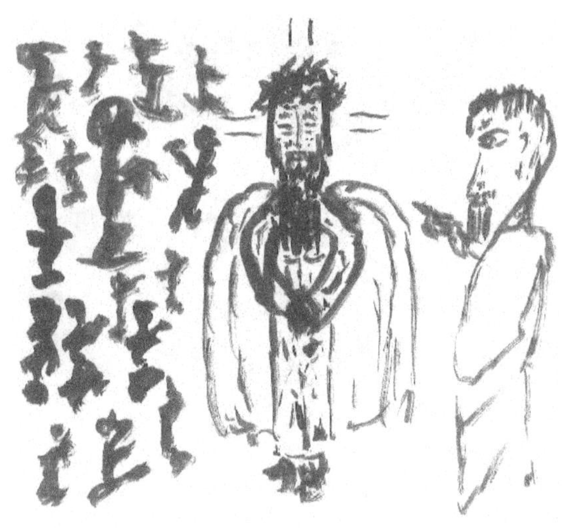

Pilate says, *Behold the Man!* The Crowds Cry, *Crucify Him!*

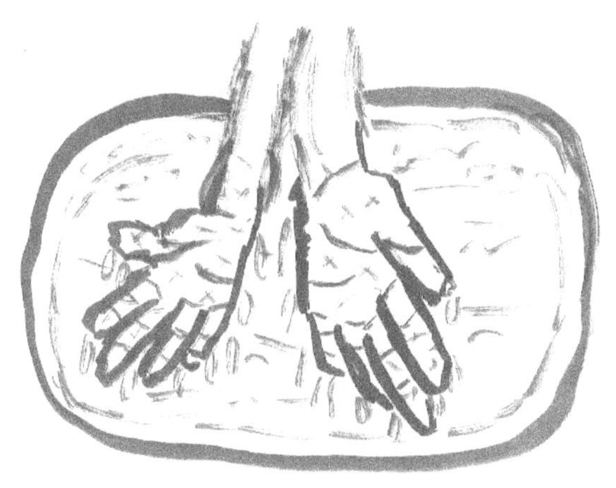

Pilate
Washes his Hands

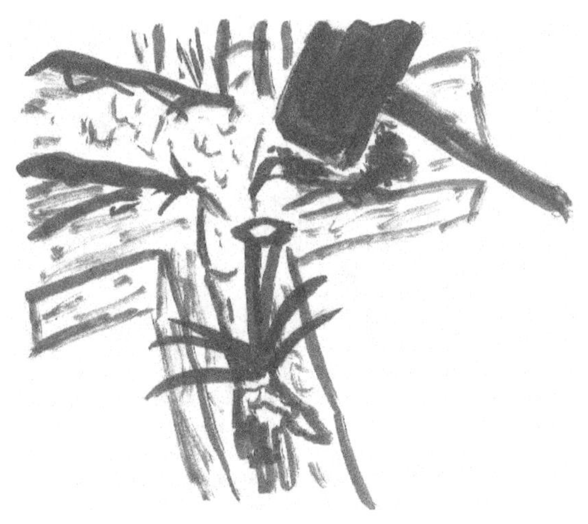

Jesus Is
Nailed Alive to a
Great Wooden Cross

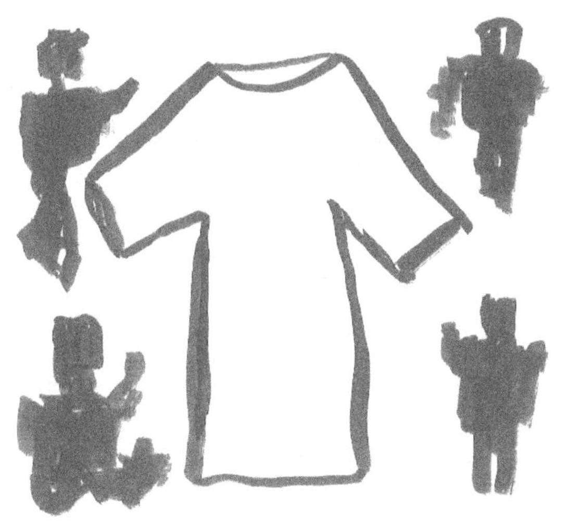

Four Soldiers Divide Jesus' Clothes and Cast Lots for His Coat

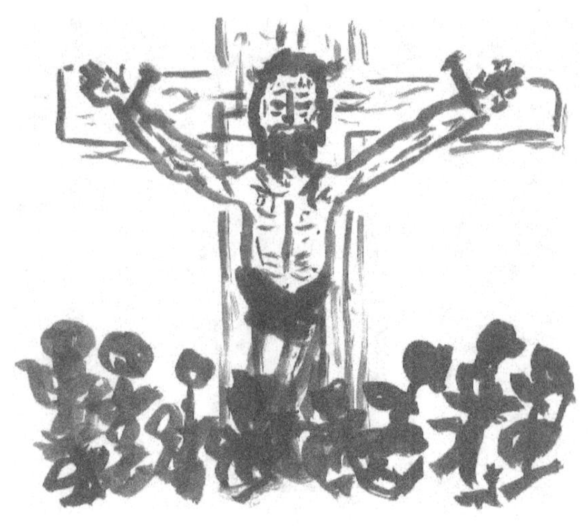

People
Who Pass That Way
Mock Him

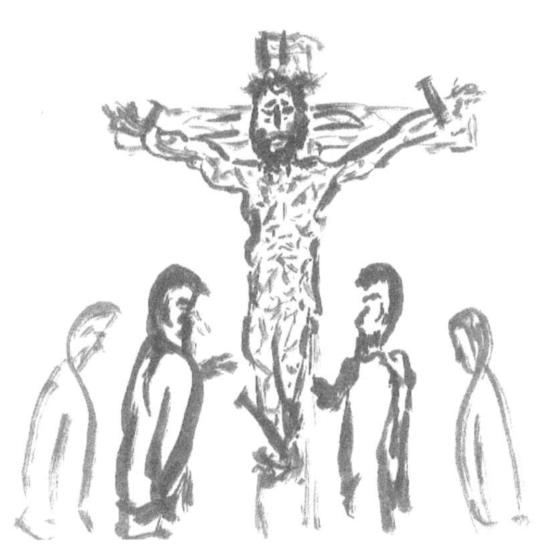

John the Beloved and
Four Women Stay,
including Mary

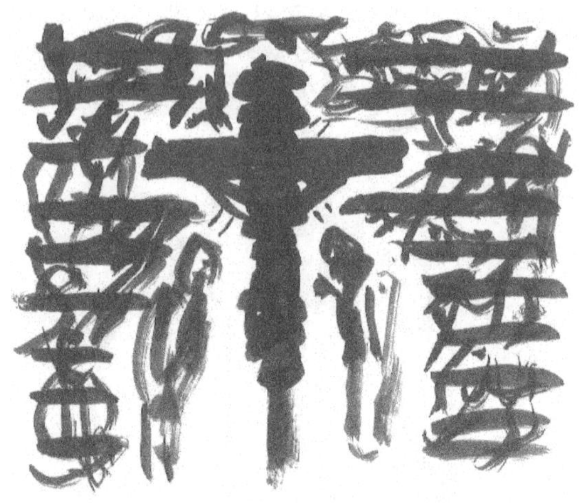

Deep Terrible Darkness Over the Whole Land

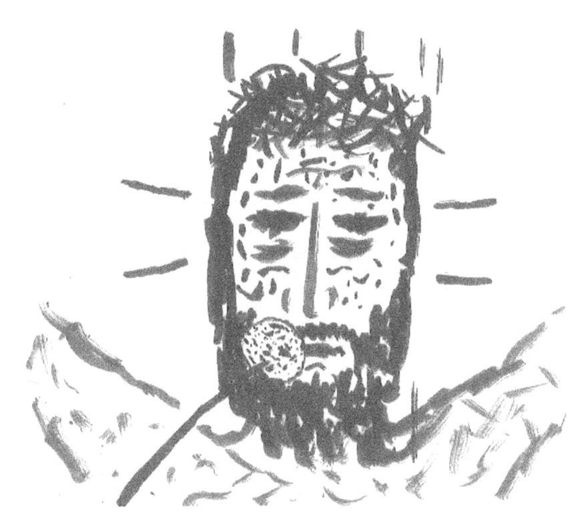

Soldiers Put to Jesus' Mouth a Sponge Dipped in Vinegar

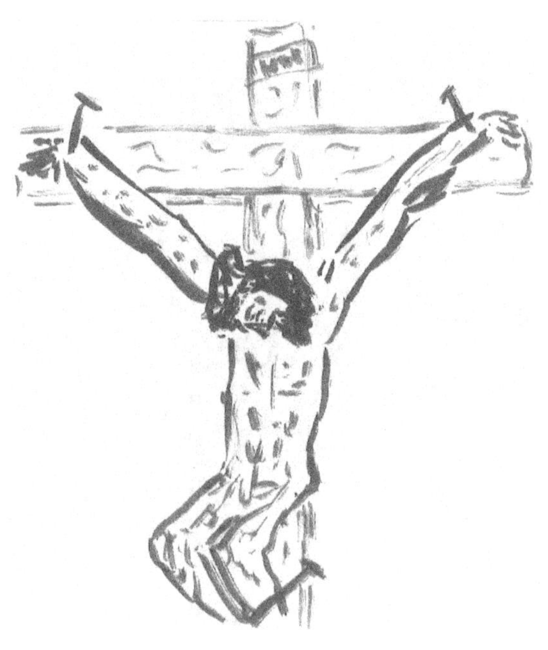

It Is Finished

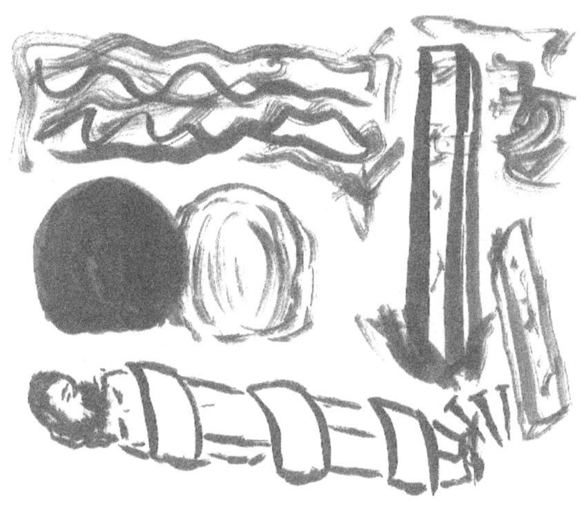

Joseph & Nicodemus Wrap & Bury the Body in a New Tomb

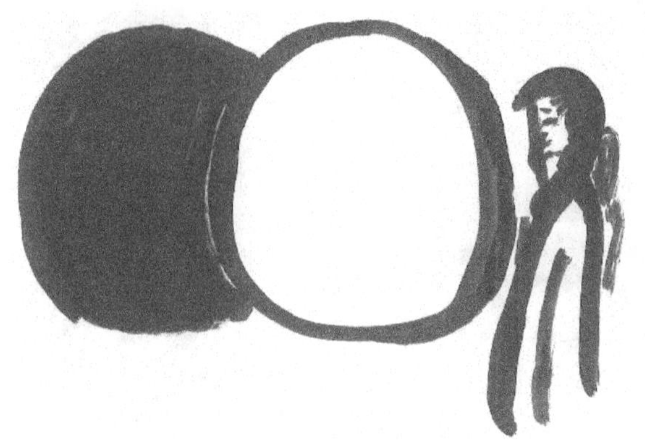

Mary Magdalene
Sees the Stone
Rolled Away

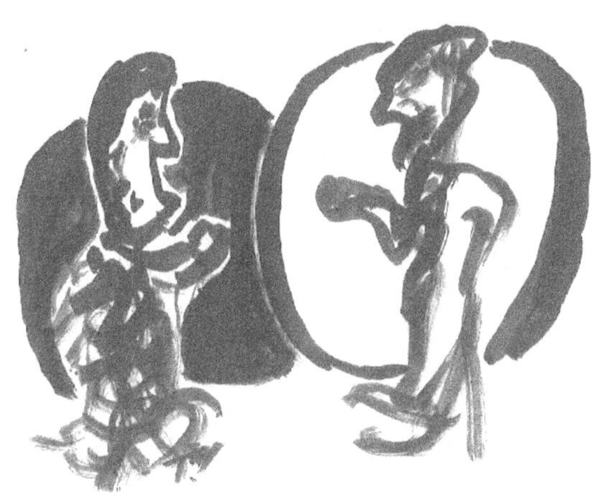

John the Beloved and Peter Go Into the Empty Tomb

Going to Emmaus a Walking Stranger Explains Scripture

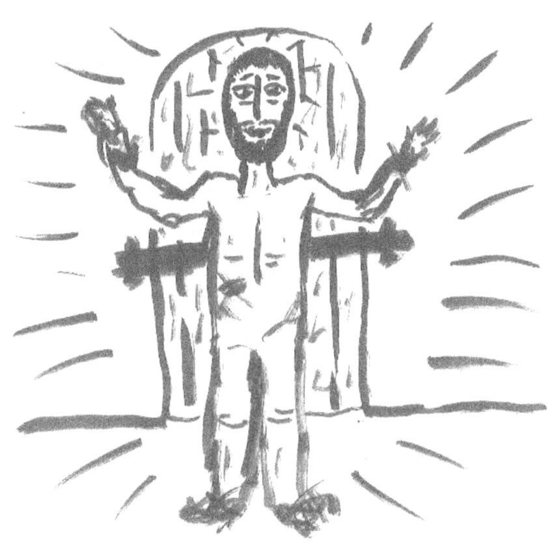

Jesus Shows Them His Hands & His Feet